St. Louis Cardinals IQ: The Ultimate Test of True Fandom

Larry Underwood

2011 Edition
(Volume II)

This title is part of the IQ sports trivia book series, which is a trademark of Black Mesa Publishing, LLC.

Cataloging-in-Publication Data is available from the Library of Congress.

ISBN: 978-0-9837922-5-3
First edition, first printing.

Cover photo courtesy of Tim Lindenbaum.

Black Mesa Publishing, LLC
Florida
David Horne and Marc CB Maxwell
Black.Mesa.Publishing@gmail.com

www.blackmesabooks.com

St. Louis Cardinals IQ

Contents

"People ask me what I do in winter when there's no baseball. I'll tell you what I do. I stare out the window and wait for spring."
— Rogers Hornsby

Introduction

THE ST. LOUIS CARDINALS; if you're a fan of this storied franchise, you probably love the game of baseball more than the average fan, and you probably know just a little bit more about the game of baseball than the average fan. That's why Cardinals fans heartily cheer the successful sacrifice bunt; or the ground ball to second base which advances a runner to third base; or an outfielder hitting the cutoff man perfectly, to help nail a speedy enemy runner at the plate. These little nuances of the game are what make the game so perfect; and very few fans of Major League Baseball appreciate these little things like Cardinals fans.

St. Louis Cardinals fans also appreciate the wonderful heritage the franchise has created, from generation to generation; from the hitting exploits of Sunny Jim Bottomley, to the wacky antics of Dizzy Dean, to quiet greatness of Stan the Man Musial, to the fierce competitiveness of Bob Gibson, to the exciting and fleet footed Lou Brock, and finally, to the current superstar of the game, the incredible Albert Pujols. We love them all, and we cherish their great accomplishments; this is the second volume of *The Ultimate Test of True Fandom*, because just one volume isn't enough to celebrate the exploits of our Redbird heroes.

Enjoy another trip down memory lane as you try to answer more than 200 questions that I've assembled for you; relax, it's a multiple choice test, broken down in ten separate "innings" (nine just wasn't enough). It's in chronological order, beginning when the franchise enjoyed its early "glory years", as an elite team in the old American Association (winning four consecutive pennants in the 1880s), continuing through several "lean" decades, until the team's first National League pennant and World Series championship (1926), and running rampant through the generations, netting 18 pennants and a National League leading 11 World Series titles (only the Yankees have more).

It's going to be a wild ride, Cardinals fans! Good luck as you test your true fandom with this latest challenge. Let's get started!

Larry Underwood
Scottsdale, Arizona
September 2011

"Players who stand flat-footed and swing with their arms are golfers, not hitters."
— *Rogers Hornsby*

First

ST. LOUIS WAS one of the six original members of the American Association, which existed as a major league from 1882 through 1891. They were also the class of this new league, winning four consecutive pennants (1885-1888); they also finished second on three different occasions (1883, 1889, and 1891), before entering a long period of mediocrity (at best) which wouldn't end until the team won its first National League pennant in 1926. Capping off that great season, the Cardinals beat the heavily favored New York Yankees in the World Series. This first inning will test your knowledge of St. Louis Cardinals history from 1882 through 1925. We're going to start off with some ancient history which will test even the most diehard Cardinals historians. Good luck!

TOP OF THE FIRST

QUESTION 1: Who was the original owner of the Cardinals?
  a) Charlie Comiskey
  b) Chris Von der Ahe
  c) Andrew Van Slyke
  d) Zeke Bonura

QUESTION 2: Name the field manager who led the Cardinals to four consecutive American Association pennants during the 1880s.
  a) Ned Cuthbert
  b) Ted Sullivan
  c) Jimmy Williams
  d) Charlie Comiskey

QUESTION 3: Name the player who posted the highest batting average for the Cardinals during the 1880s.
  a) Arlie Latham
  b) Tip O'Neill

    c)   Hugh Nicol
    d)   Bill Gleason

QUESTION 4: Name the player who led the Cardinals with 829 runs scored during the 1880s.
    a)   Arlie Latham
    b)   Bill Gleason
    c)   Tip O'Neill
    d)   Yank Robinson

QUESTION 5: What pitcher recorded the most wins for the Cardinals during the 1880s?
    a)   Silver King
    b)   Jumbo McGinnis
    c)   Bob Caruthers
    d)   Dave Fouts

QUESTION 6: How many wins did the pitching team leader collect during the 1880s?
    a)   94
    b)   104
    c)   114
    d)   217

QUESTION 7: What team did the Cardinals defeat in the 1886 World Series, to become World Champions?
    a)   Cleveland Spiders
    b)   Chicago White Stockings
    c)   Boston Red Stockings
    d)   New York Highlanders

QUESTION 8: How many runs did the Cardinals score during the 1887 season?
    a)   1,031
    b)   1,131
    c)   1,213
    d)   1,311

QUESTION 9: After winning four consecutive pennants, the Cardinals finished second to what team in 1889?
- a) Chicago Cubs
- b) Brooklyn Dodgers
- c) New York Giants
- d) Boston Braves

QUESTION 10: In 1899, what two brothers formed the new ownership for the Cardinals?
- a) Frank and Stewart Robinson
- b) Stanley and Fred Livingston
- c) Stanley and Frank Robison
- d) Frank and Brooks Robinson

Top of the First Answer Key

___ **Question 1:** B
___ **Question 2:** D
___ **Question 3:** B
___ **Question 4:** A
___ **Question 5:** D
___ **Question 6:** C
___ **Question 7:** B
___ **Question 8:** B
___ **Question 9:** B
___ **Question 10:** C

Keep a running tally of your correct answers!

Number correct: __ / 10

Overall correct: __ / 10

BOTTOM OF THE FIRST

QUESTION 11: How many times did the Cardinals finish in last place during the first decade of the 2oth century?
    a) 3
    b) 2
    c) 4
    d) 5

QUESTION 12: Owning the worst team in the National League apparently took its toll on the Robison brothers; Frank died suddenly, in 1908, and three years later, Stanley suffered an untimely death, as well.   Who took over the team upon Stanley's demise?
    a) Margaret Chase Smith
    b) Janis Robison Joplin
    c) Helene Curtis Robison
    d) Helene Robison Britton

QUESTION 13: Before the 1917 season, ownership once again transferred to someone else. Who was the new lucky owner?
    a) James Jones
    b) Edward Jones
    c) Thomas Jones
    d) Jonas Edwards

QUESTION 14: Who was hired in 1917, to help run the team's front office?
    a) Roger Bresnahan
    b) Miller Huggins
    c) Mike Gonzalez
    d) Branch Rickey

QUESTION 15: What minor league player and future Hall of Fame member did the Cardinals purchase in 1915?
    a) Jim Bottomley
    b) Rogers Hornsby

c) Miller Huggins
d) Grover Alexander

QUESTION 16: By 1920, the Cardinals had yet another owner, who also took over the presidency of the club. Who was this person?
a) Jack Stewart
b) Dick Robson
c) Sam Breadon
d) Mark Harnden

QUESTION 17: Name the recent high school graduate the Cardinals signed in 1923 who would become one of the team's great outfielders during his career.
a) Taylor Douthit
b) Chick Hafey
c) Jack Smith
d) Ray Blades

QUESTION 18: What was Rogers Hornsby's batting average in 1924?
a) .412
b) .420
c) .424
d) .418

QUESTION 19: In 1925, what Cardinals player tied a club record for most extra base hits in a game (four), with two home runs and two doubles?
a) Rogers Hornsby
b) Jim Bottomley
c) Ray Blades
d) Les Bell

QUESTION 20: Who replaced Branch Rickey as field manager of the Cardinals during the 1925 season?

a) Frank Frisch
b) Heinie Mueller
c) Rogers Hornsby
d) Bob O'Farrell

Bottom of the First Answer Key

___ **Question 11:** A
___ **Question 12:** D
___ **Question 13:** A
___ **Question 14:** D
___ **Question 15:** B
___ **Question 16:** C
___ **Question 17:** B
___ **Question 18:** C
___ **Question 19:** D
___ **Question 20:** C

Keep a running tally of your correct answers!

Number correct: __ / 10

Overall correct: __ / 20

"Let the teachers teach English and I will teach baseball. There is a lot of people in the United States who say isn't, and they ain't eating."
— Dizzy Dean

Second

BEGINNING WITH THEIR first "official" World Series championship in 1926, the Cardinals consistently fielded a competitive team that was usually in the hunt for postseason play. This inning will test your knowledge on Redbird history from 1926 through 1936 – a very colorful period of Cardinals baseball, to say the least!

TOP OF THE SECOND

QUESTION 21: What future Hall of Fame pitcher did the Cardinals acquire in June of 1926 from the Chicago Cubs?
   a) Three Finger Brown
   b) Jesse Haines
   c) Grover Alexander
   d) Dizzy Dean

QUESTION 22: Name the player who came over from the New York Giants in a trade prior to the start of the 1927 season.
   a) Frankie Frisch
   b) Specs Toporcer
   c) Heinie Schulte
   d) Rabbit Maranville

QUESTION 23: What player was dealt to the Giants in the aforementioned trade?
   a) Jim Bottomley
   b) Billy Southworth
   c) Rogers Hornsby
   d) Chick Hafey

QUESTION 24: Who played in a National League record eight World Series during his career?
   a) Rogers Hornsby
   b) Jim Bottomley

c) Frankie Frisch
d) Grover Alexander

QUESTION 25: Who led the National League with 136 RBIs and 362 total bases in 1928?
a) Rogers Hornsby
b) Jim Bottomley
c) Chick Hafey
d) Frankie Frisch

QUESTION 26: Name the pitcher who won 21 games for the Cardinals in 1928.
a) Wild Bill Hallahan
b) Jesse Haines
c) Flint Rhem
d) Bill Sherdel

QUESTION 27: Name the pitcher who led the National League with 19 wins in 1931.
a) Wild Bill Hallahan
b) Dizzy Dean
c) Jesse Haines
d) Lon Warneke

QUESTION 28: Who had 12 hits in 24 at bats in the 1931 World Series?
a) Frankie Frisch
b) Pepper Martin
c) Joe Medwick
d) George Watkins

QUESTION 29: Name the 20-year-old pitcher who made his major league debut on the last day of the 1930 season, allowing just three hits in a 3-1 victory over Pittsburgh.
a) Paul Dean
b) Paul Derringer

c) Dizzy Dean
d) Syl Johnson

QUESTION 30: Dizzy Dean won 30 games for the Cardinals in 1934, and even though they were not an official statistic at the time, he also chipped in with a few saves. Using today's rules, how many saves did he tally?
   a) 4
   b) 5
   c) 6
   d) 7

Top of the Second Answer Key

___ **Question 21:** C
___ **Question 22:** A
___ **Question 23:** C
___ **Question 24:** C
___ **Question 25:** B
___ **Question 26:** D
___ **Question 27:** A
___ **Question 28:** B
___ **Question 29:** C
___ **Question 30:** D

Keep a running tally of your correct answers!

Number correct: ___ / 10

Overall correct: ___ / 30

BOTTOM OF THE SECOND

QUESTION 31: Who hit .333 with 35 home runs and 128 RBIs for the Cardinals in 1934?
- a) Joe Medwick
- b) Ripper Collins
- c) Frankie Frisch
- d) Jack Rothrock

QUESTION 32: Who had 40 doubles for the Cardinals in 1933?
- a) Frankie Frisch
- b) Pepper Martin
- c) Ripper Collins
- d) Joe Medwick

QUESTION 33: Who led the Cardinals with a .312 batting average in 1932?
- a) Frankie Frisch
- b) George Watkins
- c) Jim Bottomley
- d) Ripper Collins

QUESTION 34: Who led the Cardinals with 18 home runs in 1933?
- a) Ripper Collins
- b) Joe Medwick
- c) George Watkins
- d) Ernie Orsatti

QUESTION 35: Who became the regular centerfielder for the Cardinals in 1935?
- a) Terry Moore
- b) Ernie Orsatti
- c) Jack Rothrock
- d) Leo Durocher

QUESTION 36: Again using today's rules, how many saves did Dizzy Dean record in 1936?
- a) 11
- b) 10
- c) 9
- d) 8

QUESTION 37: Who was the starting pitcher for the National League in the 1933 All-Star Game?
- a) Dizzy Dean
- b) Wild Bill Hallahan
- c) Bill Walker
- d) Jesse Haines

QUESTION 38: Who was the starting pitcher for the National League in the 1935 All-Star Game?
- a) Jesse Haines
- b) Wild Bill Hallahan
- c) Bill Walker
- d) Dizzy Dean

QUESTION 39: Who was the starting pitcher for the National League in the 1936 All-Star Game?
- a) Bill Walker
- b) Dizzy Dean
- c) Wild Bill Hallahan
- d) Paul Dean

QUESTION 40: Who hit 19 home runs as a rookie for the Cardinals in 1936?
- a) Terry Moore
- b) Bruce Ogrodowski
- c) Art Garibaldi
- d) Johnny Mize

BOTTOM OF THE SECOND ANSWER KEY

__ QUESTION 31: B
__ QUESTION 32: D
__ QUESTION 33: B
__ QUESTION 34: B
__ QUESTION 35: A
__ QUESTION 36: A
__ QUESTION 37: B
__ QUESTION 38: C
__ QUESTION 39: B
__ QUESTION 40: D

KEEP A RUNNING TALLY OF YOUR CORRECT ANSWERS!

Number correct: __ / 10

Overall correct: __ / 40

*"He could have hit .300 with a
fountain pen."
— Joe Garagiola, speaking about
Stan Musial*

Third

FROM 1937 THROUGH 1947, the Cardinals went to the World Series four times, winning on three of those occasions. It's no coincidence that the career of Stan Musial began right about the time the Redbirds where enjoying their most prolific period of success. Have fun reliving some wonderful Cardinals memories in this inning!

TOP OF THE THIRD

QUESTION 41: Who led the National League with a .374 batting average in 1937?
 a) Jimmy Brown
 b) Don Gutteridge
 c) Johnny Mize
 d) Joe Medwick

QUESTION 42: Who led the Cardinals with a .427 on base percentage in 1937?
 a) Jimmy Brown
 b) Don Gutteridge
 c) Johnny Mize
 d) Joe Medwick

QUESTION 43: Name the player who led the National League in home runs in 1937.
 a) Johnny Mize
 b) Joe Medwick
 c) Terry Moore
 d) Frenchy Bordagaray

QUESTION 44: How many home runs did the aforementioned player hit in 1937?
 a) 42
 b) 31

c) 39
d) 35

QUESTION 45: How many more games did Dizzy Dean win in his career, after the 1937 All-Star Game?
    a) 7
    b) 23
    c) 17
    d) 33

QUESTION 46: What significant event happened to Dizzy Dean in the 1937 All-Star Game?
    a) A line drive off the bat of Earl Averill broke his fibula
    b) Actually, that line drive shattered his kneecap
    c) Come to think of it, that line drive broke his middle toe
    d) Hold on now, that line drive broke his big toe

QUESTION 47: What team was Dizzy Dean traded to on April 16, 1938?
    a) St. Louis Browns
    b) Brooklyn Dodgers
    c) New York Giants
    d) Chicago Cubs

QUESTION 48: Dizzy Dean officially ended his major league career with what team?
    a) St. Louis Browns
    b) Chicago Cubs
    c) New York Giants
    d) Brooklyn Dodgers

QUESTION 49: Who led the National League with 52 doubles in 1939?
    a) Johnny Mize
    b) Enos Slaughter
    c) Joe Medwick
    d) Terry Moore

QUESTION 50: Name the Redbird hurler who pitched a one-hit shutout in his 1941 major league debut.
- a) Ernie White
- b) Mort Cooper
- c) Max Lanier
- d) Hank Gornicki

TOP OF THE THIRD ANSWER KEY

___ **QUESTION 41:** D
___ **QUESTION 42:** C
___ **QUESTION 43:** B
___ **QUESTION 44:** B
___ **QUESTION 45:** C
___ **QUESTION 46:** D
___ **QUESTION 47:** D
___ **QUESTION 48:** A
___ **QUESTION 49:** B
___ **QUESTION 50:** D

KEEP A RUNNING TALLY OF YOUR CORRECT ANSWERS!

Number correct: ___ / 10

Overall correct: ___ / 50

Bottom of the Third

QUESTION 51: Who led the Cardinals with 13 home runs in 1942?
- a) Enos Slaughter
- b) Stan Musial
- c) Whitey Kurowski
- d) Ray Sanders

QUESTION 52: Who led the Cardinals with 100 runs scored in 1942?
- a) Stan Musial
- b) Enos Slaughter
- c) Terry Moore
- d) Creepy Crespi

QUESTION 53: The Cardinals led the National League with 755 runs scored in 1942. How many home runs did the team hit that year?
- a) 57
- b) 76
- c) 60
- d) 67

QUESTION 54: Who led the Cardinals with 20 home runs in 1944?
- a) Stan Musial
- b) Whitey Kurowski
- c) Ray Sanders
- d) Walker Cooper

QUESTION 55: Marty Marion won the NL Most Valuable Player Award in 1944. What was his batting average that year?
- a) .302
- b) .289
- c) .275
- d) .267

QUESTION 56: What pitcher led the National League with seven shutouts in 1944?
   a) Mort Cooper
   b) Max Lanier
   c) Harry Brecheen
   d) Ted Wilks

QUESTION 57: Name the misguided Cardinals pitcher who left the team on May 23, 1944 – with a 6-0 record – to play in the newly formed Mexican League.
   a) Lou Klein
   b) Freddie Martin
   c) Murry Dickson
   d) Max Lanier

QUESTION 58: In 1947, who led the Cardinals with 27 home runs and 104 RBIs?
   a) Enos Slaughter
   b) Stan Musial
   c) Whitey Kurowski
   d) Erv Dusak

QUESTION 59: That same year, who led the Cardinals with 113 runs scored?
   a) Stan Musial
   b) Enos Slaughter
   c) Whitey Kurowski
   d) Terry Moore

QUESTION 60: Red Schoendienst led the Cardinals in stolen bases in 1947. How many bases did he steal?
   a) 14
   b) 11
   c) 23
   d) 6

Bottom of the Third Answer Key

___ **Question 51:** A
___ **Question 52:** B
___ **Question 53:** C
___ **Question 54:** B
___ **Question 55:** D
___ **Question 56:** A
___ **Question 57:** D
___ **Question 58:** C
___ **Question 59:** A
___ **Question 60:** D

Keep a running tally of your correct answers!

Number correct: ___ / 10

Overall correct: ___ / 60

*"I love to play this game of baseball.
I love putting on this uniform."*
— *Stan Musial*

Fourth

THE CARDINALS FELL on hard times in this inning, which spans from 1948 through 1958. Many of the team's productive players from the early to mid-1940s had either been traded to other teams or their skills had eroded due to age. Still, there were some memorable individual accomplishments worth noting, along with a change of ownership sponsored by the King of Beers!

TOP OF THE FOURTH

QUESTION 61: Stan Musial nearly won the 1948 NL Triple Crown; falling just one home run short of accomplishing this feat. How many home runs did "The Man" hit that year?
- a) 37
- b) 39
- c) 38
- d) 36

QUESTION 62: What two players led the NL with 13 triples in 1949?
- a) Nippy Jones & Stan Musial
- b) Stan Musial & Enos Slaughter
- c) Red Schoendienst & Stan Musial
- d) Enos Slaughter & Red Schoendienst

QUESTION 63: Whose 14th inning home run won the 1950 All-Star Game for the National League?
- a) Enos Slaughter
- b) Stan Musial
- c) Marty Marion
- d) Red Schoendienst

QUESTION 64: Who led the NL with 12 triples in 1951?
- a) Red Schoendienst
- b) Enos Slaughter

c) Stan Musial
d) Solly Hemus

QUESTION 65: Prior to the start of the 1952 season, the Cardinals traded Chuck Diering and Max Lanier to the Giants in exchange for whom?
a) Del Rice
b) Dick Sisler
c) Peanuts Lowrey
d) Eddie Stanky

QUESTION 66: Name the pitcher who led the Cardinals with 17 wins in 1952.
a) Gerry Staley
b) Vinegar Bend Mizell
c) Harry Brecheen
d) Al Brazle

QUESTION 67: In 1953, an 18-year-old Cardinals rookie hit a home run, making him the youngest player in club history to accomplish this feat. Who hit this historic shot?
a) Wally Moon
b) Steve Bilko
c) Harry Elliott
d) Dick Schofield

QUESTION 68: Just before the start of the 1954 season, the Cardinals acquired Bill Virdon, Mel Wright, and Emil Tellinger from the Yankees in exchange for whom?
a) Rip Repulski
b) Ray Jablonski
c) Enos Slaughter
d) Vic Raschi

QUESTION 69: In 1954, the first African American player made his debut for the Cardinals. Who was he?

a) Memo Luna
b) Gordon Jones
c) George Crowe
d) Tom Alston

QUESTION 70: In 1954, Jack Buck and another announcer, who would only last the one season in St. Louis, joined Harry Caray in the broadcast booth. Name this broadcaster.
a) Joe Garagiola
b) Milo Hamilton
c) Ross Porter
d) Ralph Kiner

TOP OF THE FOURTH ANSWER KEY

___ **QUESTION 61:** B
___ **QUESTION 62:** B
___ **QUESTION 63:** D
___ **QUESTION 64:** C
___ **QUESTION 65:** D
___ **QUESTION 66:** A
___ **QUESTION 67:** D
___ **QUESTION 68:** C
___ **QUESTION 69:** D
___ **QUESTION 70:** B

KEEP A RUNNING TALLY OF YOUR CORRECT ANSWERS!

Number correct: ___ / 10

Overall correct: ___ / 70

BOTTOM OF THE FOURTH

QUESTION 71: Name the first African American pitcher in Cardinals history, who made his debut in 1954.
  a) Lawrence Brooks
  b) Bob Gibson
  c) Brooks Lawrence
  d) Gibby Roberts

QUESTION 72: Name the Cardinals player who set a major league record in 1954 by collecting at least two hits in ten consecutive games.
  a) Stan Musial
  b) Rip Repulski
  c) Joe Cunningham
  d) Red Schoendienst

QUESTION 73: In 1954, this Redbird rookie became the only player in major league history to hit three home runs in his first two games in the big leagues. Who did it?
  a) Sal Yvars
  b) Joe Cunningham
  c) Bill Sarni
  d) Wally Moon

QUESTION 74: What pitcher led the Cardinals with just 12 wins in 1955?
  a) Harvey Haddix
  b) Luis Arroyo
  c) Larry Jackson
  d) Tom Poholski

QUESTION 75: What rookie pitcher won 15 games for the Cardinals in 1954?
  a) Tom Poholski
  b) Gerry Staley
  c) Brooks Lawrence
  d) Gordon Jones

QUESTION 76: Name the rookie who led the Cardinals with 22 stolen bases in 1955.
- a) Bill Virdon
- b) Ken Boyer
- c) Bill Sarni
- d) Harry Elliott

QUESTION 77: In 1956, the Cardinals acquired Bobby Del Greco and Dick Littlefield from the Pirates in exchange for whom?
- a) Alex Grammas
- b) Joe Frazier
- c) Harvey Haddix
- d) Bill Virdon

QUESTION 78: Name the player who led the Cardinals with 105 RBIs in 1957.
- a) Del Ennis
- b) Stan Musial
- c) Wally Moon
- d) Ken Boyer

QUESTION 79: Name the player who led the Cardinals with 108 runs scored in 1957.
- a) Ken Boyer
- b) Stan Musial
- c) Wally Moon
- d) Don Blasingame

QUESTION 80: Name the first Cardinals pitcher to strike out at least 200 batters in a season. He did it in 1958 by recording 225 strikeouts.
- a) Bob Gibson
- b) Sam Jones
- c) Larry Jackson
- d) Lindy McDaniel

Bottom of the Fourth Answer Key

___ **Question 71:** C
___ **Question 72:** B
___ **Question 73:** B
___ **Question 74:** A
___ **Question 75:** C
___ **Question 76:** B
___ **Question 77:** D
___ **Question 78:** A
___ **Question 79:** D
___ **Question 80:** B

Keep a running tally of your correct answers!

Number correct: ___ / 10

Overall correct: ___ / 80

"The two most important things in life: good friends and a strong bullpen."
— Bob Gibson

Fifth

FROM 1959 THROUGH 1969, the Cardinals played in three separate World Series – 1964, 1967, and 1968 – winning the first two, and narrowly missing out on the last one. This inning began a period of rejuvenation for the franchise, until after the Cardinals lost the 1968 World Series, when they slowly faded into obscurity throughout the '70s and early '80s. However, during the late '50s and early '60s, the team was on the rise, as key players that would lead the team to glory were being assembled. This is most definitely a fascinating era of Cardinals baseball, filled with many great championship moments. Enjoy!

TOP OF THE FIFTH

QUESTION 81: Who led the Cardinals with a .345 batting average in 1959?
   a) Joe Cunningham
   b) Ken Boyer
   c) Don Blasingame
   d) Curt Flood

QUESTION 82: Who led the Cardinals with 28 home runs in 1959?
   a) Stan Musial
   b) Joe Cunningham
   c) Ken Boyer
   d) Bill White

QUESTION 83: Who led the Cardinals with 19 stolen bases in 1960?
   a) Ken Boyer
   b) Curt Flood
   c) Daryl Spencer
   d) Julian Javier

QUESTION 84: Which pitcher led the Cardinals with 21 wins in 1960?
- a)   Ernie Broglio
- b)   Bob Gibson
- c)   Ray Sadecki
- d)   Curt Simmons

QUESTION 85: Name the relief ace whose 26 saves in 1960 established a new Cardinals team record.
- a)   Ron Kline
- b)   Larry Jackson
- c)   Vinegar Bend Mizell
- d)   Lindy McDaniel

QUESTION 86: Name the manager who replaced Solly Hemus midway through the 1961 season.
- a)   Red Schoendienst
- b)   Fred Hutchinson
- c)   Johnny Keane
- d)   Stan Hack

QUESTION 87: Name the relief ace who appeared in 99 games for the Cardinals from 1962 to 1964, while posting a 2.51 ERA.
- a)   Barney Schultz
- b)   John Anderson
- c)   Bobby Schantz
- d)   Roger Craig

QUESTION 88: At the conclusion of the 1962 season, the Cardinals traded Don Cardwell and Julio Gotay to the Pirates in exchange for whom?
- a)   George Altman
- b)   Charlie James
- c)   Lew Burdette
- d)   Dick Groat

QUESTION 89: Who led the Cardinals with a .527 slugging percentage in 1964?

- a) Lou Brock
- b) Ken Boyer
- c) Bill White
- d) Mike Shannon

QUESTION 90: How many days did the Cardinals occupy first place in 1964?

- a) 6
- b) 5
- c) 8
- d) 9

Top of the Fifth Answer Key

___ **Question 81:** A
___ **Question 82:** C
___ **Question 83:** D
___ **Question 84:** A
___ **Question 85:** D
___ **Question 86:** C
___ **Question 87:** C
___ **Question 88:** D
___ **Question 89:** A
___ **Question 90:** A

Keep a running tally of your correct answers!

Number correct: ___ / 10

Overall correct: ___ / 90

BOTTOM OF THE FIFTH

QUESTION 91: Who played second base for the Cardinals in the 1964 World Series?
 a) Julian Javier
 b) Dal Maxvill
 c) Charlie James
 d) Dick Groat

QUESTION 92: Name the Cardinals pitcher who made his major league debut in 1965, issuing a base on balls to the only batter he faced.
 a) Dick Hughes
 b) Steve Carlton
 c) Hal Woodeshick
 d) Don Dennis

QUESTION 93: Who hit the first home run for the Cardinals in the new Busch Memorial Stadium, which opened on May 12, 1966?
 a) Orlando Cepeda
 b) Lou Brock
 c) Mike Shannon
 d) Tim McCarver

QUESTION 94: Aside from Bob Gibson, who else hit a home run for the Cardinals in Game 7 of the 1967 World Series against Boston?
 a) Orlando Cepeda
 b) Lou Brock
 c) Mike Shannon
 d) Julian Javier

QUESTION 95: Who led the NL with 12 triples in 1968?
 a) Tim McCarver
 b) Lou Brock

    c) Curt Flood
    d) Bobby Tolan

QUESTION 96: How many shutouts did Bob Gibson record in 1968?
    a) 12
    b) 14
    c) 10
    d) 13

QUESTION 97: Name the pitcher who won 19 games for the Cardinals in 1968.
    a) Steve Carlton
    b) Nelson Briles
    c) Ray Washburn
    d) Larry Jaster

QUESTION 98: Who hit the only home run in Game1 of the 1968 World Series?
    a) Mike Shannon
    b) Tim McCarver
    c) Orlando Cepeda
    d) Lou Brock

QUESTION 99: Name the relief pitcher who led both the 1967 and 1968 pennant winners in games pitched.
    a) Joe Hoerner
    b) Ron Willis
    c) Al Jackson
    d) Larry Jaster

QUESTION 100: Name the pitcher who made his major league debut for the Cardinals on September 27, 1969, allowing just two hits and no runs in seven innings of work.
    a) Mike Torrez
    b) Frank Linzy

c) Chuck Taylor
d) Jerry Reuss

BOTTOM OF THE FIFTH ANSWER KEY

___ **QUESTION 91:** B
___ **QUESTION 92:** B
___ **QUESTION 93:** B
___ **QUESTION 94:** D
___ **QUESTION 95:** B
___ **QUESTION 96:** D
___ **QUESTION 97:** B
___ **QUESTION 98:** D
___ **QUESTION 99:** B
___ **QUESTION 100:** D

KEEP A RUNNING TALLY OF YOUR CORRECT ANSWERS!

Number correct: ___ / 10

Overall correct: ___ / 100

"Lefty was a craftsman, an artist. He was a perfectionist. He painted a ballgame. Stroke, stroke, stroke, and when he got through it was a masterpiece."
— Richie Ashburn, speaking about Steve Carlton

Sixth

FROM 1970 THROUGH 1980, the Cardinals never reached the postseason, thanks in large part to a series of ill-advised trades; most notably, sending Steve Carlton to Philadelphia and Jerry Reuss to Houston after the 1971 season. The process of age was also taking its toll on the team's World Series heroes of the '60s – Bob Gibson was forced to retire after the 1975 season, due to a bad knee; Lou Brock ended his long career in 1979, but not before passing the 3000 hit plateau in August of that year. Curt Flood and Tim McCarver were both gone before the start of the '70 season, and Mike Shannon would be forced to retire shortly thereafter, due to severe kidney problems. There were some young, rising stars on the horizon – most notably, Ted Simmons, Keith Hernandez, Bob Forsch, and Garry Templeton. Unfortunately, for the most part, they were surrounded by a mediocre supporting cast who never had what it took to experience the glory of postseason action; although they came close in 1973 and 1974, finishing just a game and a half out of first place both years.

TOP OF THE SIXTH

QUESTION 101: Name the player who collected 24 hits in 73 at-bats in 1970; all as a pinch hitter.
- a) Carl Taylor
- b) Leron Lee
- c) Vic Davalillo
- d) Jose Cardenal

QUESTION 102: Name the pitcher who lost 19 games for the Cardinals in 1970.
- a) Steve Carlton
- b) Mike Torrez
- c) Jerry Reuss
- d) Nelson Briles

QUESTION 103: Name the pitcher who led the Cardinals with 20 wins in 1971.
- a) Reggie Cleveland
- b) Jerry Reuss
- c) Bob Gibson
- d) Steve Carlton

QUESTION 104: Name the Cardinals player who collected his 2,000th career hit in 1973.
- a) Lou Brock
- b) Tim McCarver
- c) Jose Cruz
- d) Joe Torre

QUESTION 105: Name the Cardinals pitcher who led the team with 16 wins in 1974.
- a) Lynn McGlothlen
- b) John Curtis
- c) Bob Forsch
- d) Bob Gibson

QUESTION 106: Along with Reggie Smith, name the other player who led the Cardinals with a .309 batting average in 1974.
- a) Lou Brock
- b) Bake McBride
- c) Joe Torre
- d) Ted Simmons

QUESTION 107: In 1976 the Cardinals acquired Joe Ferguson and two other players from the Dodgers in exchange for whom?
- a) Willie Crawford
- b) Vic Harris
- c) Mike Anderson
- d) Reggie Smith

QUESTION 108: Name the only Cardinals player to hit over .300 in 1976.
   a) Keith Hernandez
   b) Bake McBride
   c) Lou Brock
   d) Ted Simmons

QUESTION 109: After trading Ken Reitz to the Giants in 1975 for pitcher Pete Falcone, the Cardinals reacquired Reitz after the 1976 season in exchange for whom?
   a) Willie Crawford
   b) John Curtis
   c) Bill Grief
   d) Lynn McGlothlen

QUESTION 110: Who replaced Red Schoendienst as manager of the Cardinals after the 1976 season?
   a) Jack Krol
   b) Ken Boyer
   c) Vern Rapp
   d) Dick Sisler

Top of the Sixth Answer Key

___ **Question 101:** C
___ **Question 102:** A
___ **Question 103:** D
___ **Question 104:** D
___ **Question 105:** A
___ **Question 106:** B
___ **Question 107:** D
___ **Question 108:** C
___ **Question 109:** D
___ **Question 110:** C

Keep a running tally of your correct answers!

Number correct: ___ / 10

Overall correct: ___ / 110

BOTTOM OF THE SIXTH

QUESTION 111: Who led the NL with 18 triples in 1977?
a) Lou Brock
b) Jerry Mumphrey
c) Tony Scott
d) Garry Templeton

QUESTION 112: Who replaced Vern Rapp as the *permanent* Cardinals manager in 1978, after Rapp's disgruntled squad began the season with a 6-11 record?
a) Jack Krol
b) Whitey Herzog
c) Ken Boyer
d) Charlie Smith

QUESTION 113: Who led the Cardinals with 40 doubles in 1978?
a) Garry Templeton
b) Keith Hernandez
c) Tony Scott
d) Ted Simmons

QUESTION 114: Name the Cardinals rookie pitcher who tossed a one-hitter in his major league debut in 1978, beating the Mets at Shea Stadium by the score of 8-2.
a) Eric Rasmussen
b) John Urrea
c) Buddy Schultz
d) Silvio Martinez

QUESTION 115: Who is the only player in National League history to lead the league in triples for three consecutive years?
a) Keith Hernandez
b) Tony Scott
c) Garry Templeton
d) Jerry Mumphrey

QUESTION 116: In December of 1979, the Cardinals traded John Denny and Jerry Mumphrey to Cleveland in exchange for whom?
a) George Hendrick
b) Dane Iorg
c) Pete Vuckovich
d) Bobby Bonds

QUESTION 117: Name the veteran pitcher the Cardinals purchased from the Yankees in April of 1980.
a) Mudcat Grant
b) Jim Kaat
c) Don Hood
d) Jim Bibby

QUESTION 118: What player finished second in the NL batting race in 1980 with a .321 batting average?
a) Garry Templeton
b) Ted Simmons
c) George Hendrick
d) Keith Hernandex

QUESTION 119: What player finished third in the NL batting race in 1980 with a .319 batting average?
a) Keith Hernandez
b) Ted Simmons
c) Garry Templeton
d) George Hendrick

QUESTION 120: In December of 1980, Leon Durham, Ken Reitz, and Tye Waller were traded to the Cubs in exchange for whom?
a) Tito Landrum and Larry Sorensen
b) Bob Shirley and Gene Tenace
c) Sixto Lezcano and Mike Ramsey
d) Bruce Sutter

Bottom of the Sixth Answer Key

___ **Question 111:** D
___ **Question 112:** C
___ **Question 113:** D
___ **Question 114:** D
___ **Question 115:** C
___ **Question 116:** D
___ **Question 117:** B
___ **Question 118:** D
___ **Question 119:** C
___ **Question 120:** D

Keep a running tally of your correct answers!

Number correct: ___ / 10

Overall correct: ___ / 120

"I'm not buddy-buddy with the players. If they need a buddy, let them buy a dog."
— Whitey Herzog

Seventh

THIS INNING **(1981-1991)** will celebrate the exciting style of play and tremendous success engineered by the one and only Whitey Herzog, who guided the Redbirds to three trips to the World Series during his reign; winning once (in thrilling fashion) while losing twice (in heartbreaking fashion). However, by the end of Herzog's remarkable tenure at the helm of the Cardinals, his team had changed, for the worse; resigning before the 1990 All-Star break, it's clear he knew the team was going nowhere, so he got out while the getting was good. By season's end, the Cardinals had finished in the NL East cellar; several seasons of lackluster performance for the franchise would follow, before a change in team ownership and another new field manager would help turn things around. First things first; are you ready for some "Whitey Ball"? Let's get started!

TOP OF THE SEVENTH

QUESTION 121: In June of 1981, the Cardinals traded outfielder Tony Scott to the Houston Astros in exchange for whom?
    a) Jose Cruz
    b) Joaquin Andujar
    c) Kevin Bass
    d) Orlando Sanchez

QUESTION 122: Name the 1982 NL leader in runs scored (120).
    a) Lonnie Smith
    b) Willie McGee
    c) George Hendrick
    d) Keith Hernandez

QUESTION 123: What was the longest winning streak the Cardinals had in 1982?
    a) 12 games
    b) 13 games

c) 11 games

d) 10 games

QUESTION 124: *Before clinching the division title,* what was the longest losing streak the Cardinals had in 1982?

a) 3 games

b) 4 games

c) 5 games

d) 6 games

QUESTION 125: In the 1982 World Series, who drove in the tying runs in the bottom of the sixth inning of Game 7, when the Cardinals were trailing 3-1?

a) Darrell Porter

b) Keith Hernandez

c) Lonnie Smith

d) George Hendrick

QUESTION 126: Who drove in the go-head run in Game 7 of the 1982 World Series for the Cardinals?

a) George Hendrick

b) Lonnie Smith

c) Keith Hernandez

d) Darrell Porter

QUESTION 127: Name the Cardinals pitcher who threw ten shutout innings in his August 1983 major league debut.

a) Joe Magrane

b) Kurt Kepshire

c) Danny Cox

d) Ricky Horton

QUESTION 128: Who was the National League's only 20 game winner in 1984?

a) Danny Cox

b) Kurt Kepshire

c) Dave LaPoint
d) Joaquin Andujar

QUESTION 129: In December of 1984, the Cardinals traded George Hendrick and Steve Barnard to the Pirates in exchange for Brian Harper and another player. Who was the other player?
a) Ken Dayley
b) Tito Landrum
c) Tom Nieto
d) John Tudor

QUESTION 130: Who won 18 games for the Cardinals in 1985?
a) Joaquin Andujar
b) Danny Cox
c) John Tudor
d) Bob Forsch

TOP OF THE SEVENTH ANSWER KEY

___ **QUESTION 121:** B
___ **QUESTION 122:** A
___ **QUESTION 123:** A
___ **QUESTION 124:** A
___ **QUESTION 125:** B
___ **QUESTION 126:** A
___ **QUESTION 127:** C
___ **QUESTION 128:** D
___ **QUESTION 129:** D
___ **QUESTION 130:** B

KEEP A RUNNING TALLY OF YOUR CORRECT ANSWERS!

Number correct: ___ / 10

Overall correct: ___ / 130

BOTTOM OF THE SEVENTH

QUESTION 131: Name the relief pitcher who led the Cardinals with 19 saves in 1985.
  a) Ricky Horton
  b) Ken Dayley
  c) Jeff Lahti
  d) Todd Worrell

QUESTION 132: How many home runs did Jack Clark hit in 1985?
  a) 20
  b) 22
  c) 24
  d) 21

QUESTION 133: How many home runs did Jack Clark hit in 1987?
  a) 31
  b) 29
  c) 35
  d) 32

QUESTION 134: Who led the Cardinals with 33 saves in 1987?
  a) Ricky Horton
  b) Ken Dayley
  c) Todd Worrell
  d) Pat Perry

QUESTION 135: Bob Forsch, Danny Cox, and Greg Mathews tied for the team lead in victories for the Cardinals in 1987. How many did each pitcher tally?
  a) 15
  b) 16
  c) 11
  d) 12

QUESTION 136: Joe Magrane won the National League ERA title in 1988 with a figure of 2.18; how many games did he win that season?
    a) 14
    b) 19
    c) 10
    d) 5

QUESTION 137: In 1988, the Cardinals traded John Tudor to the Dodgers in exchange for whom?
    a) Milt Thompson
    b) Pedro Guerrero
    c) Jose DeLeon
    d) Ken Hill

QUESTION 138: Name the pitcher who led the National League with 201 strikeouts in 1989.
    a) Joe Magrane
    b) Jose DeLeon
    c) Ken Hill
    d) Scott Terry

QUESTION 139: In 1990, the Cardinals acquired Lee Smith from the Red Sox in exchange for whom?
    a) Alex Cole and Steve Peters
    b) Willie McGee
    c) Terry Pendleton
    d) Tom Brunansky

QUESTION 140: Todd Zeile led the Cardinals in home runs in 1991. What was his total?
    a) 19
    b) 11
    c) 14
    d) 15

BOTTOM OF THE SEVENTH ANSWER KEY

___ QUESTION 131: C
___ QUESTION 132: B
___ QUESTION 133: C
___ QUESTION 134: A
___ QUESTION 135: C
___ QUESTION 136: D
___ QUESTION 137: B
___ QUESTION 138: B
___ QUESTION 139: D
___ QUESTION 140: B

KEEP A RUNNING TALLY OF YOUR CORRECT ANSWERS!

Number correct: ___ / 10

Overall correct: ___ / 140

"What a perfect way to end the home stand, by hitting 62 for the city of St. Louis and all the fans. I truly wanted to do it here and I did. Thank you St. Louis."
— Mark McGwire, September 8, 1998, after surpassing Roger Maris' home run record

Eighth

FROM 1992 THROUGH 2002, the Cardinals slowly transformed from a team that relied greatly on speed to generate offense, to one that was more home run oriented. The '90s produced just one divisional winner – the '96 team that came within one postseason victory from a World Series engagement. Alas, after taking a 3-1 NLCS lead over Atlanta, the Cardinals were clobbered by the Braves the next three games. The following season, the Cardinals did little to generate excitement, until the late season acquisition of slugger Mark McGwire from Oakland. His playing days in St. Louis were somewhat limited – a bad knee forced his retirement after the 2000 season – but his impact on the game and the excitement he created for Cardinals fans during his brief stay was astounding. With McGwire's exit from the game, a new source of excitement was delivered when rookie Albert Pujols broke in with the Redbirds in 2001. Not coincidentally, the Cardinals made postseason appearances in '01 and '02, losing in the first round to the Arizona Diamondbacks, and then falling to the Giants in the following year's NLCS. The future for the Cardinals, of course, would only be brighter.

TOP OF THE EIGHTH

QUESTION 141: Name the pitcher who led the Cardinals with 16 wins in 1992.
   a) Bob Tewksbury
   b) Donovan Osborn
   c) Rheal Cormier
   d) Omar Olivares

QUESTION 142: Name the player who led the Cardinals with 46 stolen bases in 1993.
   a) Ozzie Smith
   b) Bernard Gilkey

c) Ray Lankford
d) Greg Jefferies

QUESTION 143: Name the player who led the Cardinals with 103 RBIs in 1993.
a) Mark Whiten
b) Todd Zeile
c) Gregg Jefferies
d) Ray Lankford

QUESTION 144: Name the Cardinals pitcher who started the 1994 season with seven consecutive victories.
a) Donovan Osborn
b) Rheal Cormier
c) Bob Tewksbury
d) Joe Magrane

QUESTION 145: Name the pitcher who led the Cardinals with eight measly wins in 1995.
a) Mark Petkovsek
b) Allen Watson
c) Ken Hill
d) Rich DeLucia

QUESTION 146: Name the pitcher who led the Cardinals with 18 wins in 1996.
a) Andy Benes
b) Todd Stottlemyre
c) Donovan Osborn
d) Mike Morgan

QUESTION 147: In 1997, the Cardinals had the worst start in club history. How many consecutive games did they lose to begin that dismal season?
a) 5
b) 6

c) 7

d) 8

QUESTION 148: How many home runs did Mark McGwire hit as a member of the Cardinals (1997-2000)?

a) 225

b) 230

c) 220

d) 215

QUESTION 149: Who led the National League with 14 triples in 1997?

a) Royce Clayton

b) Delino DeShields

c) Ron Gant

d) Ray Lankford

QUESTION 150: How many RBIs did Mark McGwire have in 1998?

a) 149

b) 141

c) 145

d) 147

TOP OF THE EIGHTH ANSWER KEY

___ **QUESTION 141:** A
___ **QUESTION 142:** D
___ **QUESTION 143:** B
___ **QUESTION 144:** C
___ **QUESTION 145:** D
___ **QUESTION 146:** A
___ **QUESTION 147:** B
___ **QUESTION 148:** C
___ **QUESTION 149:** B
___ **QUESTION 150:** D

KEEP A RUNNING TALLY OF YOUR CORRECT ANSWERS!

Number correct: __ / 10

Overall correct: __ / 150

Bottom of the Eighth

Question 151: Before Mark McGwire's 70 home runs for the Cardinals in 1998, Johnny Mize held the club record for most home runs in a season. What was that total?
  a) 45
  b) 43
  c) 42
  d) 47

Question 152: In 1998, the Cardinals led the National League in home runs for the first time since 1944, establishing a club record in the process. How many home runs did the Redbirds tally in '98?
  a) 229
  b) 231
  c) 219
  d) 223

Question 153: On September 8, 1998 Mark McGwire hit his record breaking 62nd home run of the season off what Chicago Cubs pitcher?
  a) Mike Morgan
  b) Tim Stoddard
  c) Steve Trachsel
  d) Kerry Woods

Question 154: In 1998, Mark McGwire set a club record for most walks in a season. How many free passes did he receive that year?
  a) 159
  b) 168
  c) 164
  d) 162

QUESTION 155: How many home runs did Mark McGwire hit in 1999?
- a) 66
- b) 64
- c) 67
- d) 63

QUESTION 156: In December of 1999, the Cardinals traded Juan Acevedo and two other players to the Brewers in exchange for whom?
- a) Mike Matheny
- b) Craig Paquette
- c) Placido Polanco
- d) Fernando Vina

QUESTION 157: Name the player who set a Cardinals franchise record in 2000 by reaching base in 12 consecutive plate appearances.
- a) Fernando Vina
- b) Jim Edmonds
- c) J.D. Drew
- d) Edgar Renteria

QUESTION 158: In 2000, the Cardinals established another new club record for home runs in a single season. How many did they hit that year?
- a) 232
- b) 235
- c) 237
- d) 239

QUESTION 159: Name the Cardinals pitcher who appeared in a club record 89 games in 2001.
- a) Mike Timlin
- b) Mike Matthews
- c) Steve Kline
- d) Gene Stechschulte

QUESTION 160: Name the free agent acquisition – formerly with the Blue Jays – who was signed by the Cardinals in December of 2002.

a) Joe Girardi
b) Cal Eldred
c) Chris Carpenter
d) Eduardo Perez

Bottom of the Eighth Answer Key

___ **Question 151:** B
___ **Question 152:** D
___ **Question 153:** C
___ **Question 154:** D
___ **Question 155:** A
___ **Question 156:** D
___ **Question 157:** B
___ **Question 158:** B
___ **Question 159:** C
___ **Question 160:** C

Keep a running tally of your correct answers!

Number correct: ___ / 10

Overall correct: ___ / 160

"It's not what you did last year. It's what you're going to do this year. That's more important."
— Albert Pujols

Ninth

FROM 2003 THROUGH 2010, the Cardinals reached the postseason on four different occasions, including two World Series appearances – losing to the Red Sox in 2004 (4 games to none) and beating the Tigers in 2006 (4 games to 1). Much of that success can be attributed to the game's greatest player – Albert Pujols. His offensive production has been nothing short of amazing over the ten-year span he's been with the Cardinals. Pujols has also turned into a Gold Glove performer at first base, with remarkable agility and quickness around the bag; he not only drives in tons of runs with his bat, he saves bunches of runs with his glove. By the time his playing days are over, Albert may well be regarded as *the best to ever play the game.* Time will tell. I know I speak for millions of Cardinals fans throughout Cardinal Nation when I say, "Thanks for the great memories, Albert. We hope you stay a Cardinal for life."

TOP OF THE NINTH

QUESTION 161: In 2003, what player tied a Cardinals club record for most extra base hits in a game (four), with two homers and two doubles, *on two separate occasions*?
   a) Scott Rolen
   b) Jim Edmonds
   c) Albert Pujols
   d) J.D. Drew

QUESTION 162: Name the pitcher who started the 2003 season with a 7-0 won-loss record.
   a) Woody Williams
   b) Matt Morris
   c) Brett Tomko
   d) Garrett Stephenson

QUESTION 163: Name the player who hit safely in 30 straight games for the Cardinals in 2003.
- a) Edgar Renteria
- b) Albert Pujols
- c) Scott Rolen
- d) Fernando Vina

QUESTION 164: One other Cardinals player also has a 30-game hitting streak to his credit. Who is it?
- a) Ken Boyer
- b) Joe Medwick
- c) Curt Flood
- d) Stan Musial

QUESTION 165: What was Albert Pujols' batting average in 2003?
- a) .356
- b) .359
- c) .346
- d) .349

QUESTION 166: In December of 2003, the Cardinals traded J.D. Drew and Eli Marrero to the Braves in exchange for Jason Marquis, Ray King, and one other player; who was the other player?
- a) Tony Womack
- b) Reggie Sanders
- c) Jeff Suppan
- d) Adam Wainwright

QUESTION 167: Name the pitcher who led the Cardinals with 16 wins in 2004.
- a) Matt Morris
- b) Jeff Suppan
- c) Chris Carpenter
- d) Woody Williams

QUESTION 168: How many saves did Jason Isringhausen notch for the Cardinals in 2004?
   a) 43
   b) 48
   c) 47
   d) 41

QUESTION 169: Name the player who tied a Cardinals club record in 2004 with home runs in five straight games.
   a) Jim Edmonds
   b) Albert Pujols
   c) Scott Rolen
   d) Reggie Sanders

QUESTION 170: In December of 2004, the Cardinals traded Dan Haren and two other players to Oakland for whom?
   a) David Eckstein
   b) Mark Mulder
   c) Randy Flores
   d) John Rodriguez

Top of the Ninth Answer Key

___ **Question 161:** B
___ **Question 162:** A
___ **Question 163:** B
___ **Question 164:** D
___ **Question 165:** B
___ **Question 166:** D
___ **Question 167:** B
___ **Question 168:** C
___ **Question 169:** A
___ **Question 170:** B

Keep a running tally of your correct answers!

Number correct: __ / 10

Overall correct: __ / 170

BOTTOM OF THE NINTH

QUESTION 171: Name the player who led the Cardinals with 16 stolen bases in 2005.
   a) Mark Grudzielanek
   b) David Eckstein
   c) Reggie Sanders
   d) Albert Pujols

QUESTION 172: Name the Cardinals player who hit for the cycle in April of 2005.
   a) Jim Edmonds
   b) Scott Rolen
   c) Mark Grudzielanek
   d) Albert Pujols

QUESTION 173: How many eight-game losing streaks did the Cardinals endure in 2006?
   a) 1
   b) 2
   c) 3
   d) 0

QUESTION 174: How many seven-game losing streaks did the Cardinals endure in 2006?
   a) 1
   b) 2
   c) 3
   d) 0

QUESTION 175: Name the player who was the 2006 World Series MVP.
   a) Albert Pujols
   b) Jim Edmonds
   c) David Eckstein
   d) Scott Rolen

QUESTION 176: Name the Cardinals pitcher who began the 2007 season with ten consecutive losses.
a) Braden Looper
b) Kip Wells
c) Randy Flores
d) Anthony Reyes

QUESTION 177: Name the pitcher who led the Cardinals with 15 wins in 2008.
a) Kyle Lohse
b) Todd Wellemeyer
c) Braden Looper
d) Adam Wainwright

QUESTION 178: Name the player who tied a Cardinals club record in 2008 by hitting a home run in five consecutive games.
a) Ryan Ludwick
b) Albert Pujols
c) Troy Glaus
d) Skip Schumaker

QUESTION 179: Name the player who led the Cardinals with 16 stolen bases in 2009.
a) Brendan Ryan
b) Colby Rasmus
c) Rick Ankiel
d) Albert Pujols

QUESTION 180: What was the Cardinals' combined won-loss record against the Brewers, Cubs, and Astros in 2010?
a) 20 wins-25 losses
b) 18 wins-27 losses
c) 16 wins-29 losses
d) 21 wins-24 losses

BOTTOM OF THE NINTH ANSWER KEY

___ **QUESTION 171:** D
___ **QUESTION 172:** C
___ **QUESTION 173:** B
___ **QUESTION 174:** A
___ **QUESTION 175:** C
___ **QUESTION 176:** D
___ **QUESTION 177:** A
___ **QUESTION 178:** A
___ **QUESTION 179:** D
___ **QUESTION 180:** B

KEEP A RUNNING TALLY OF YOUR CORRECT ANSWERS!

Number correct: __ / 10

Overall correct: __ / 180

*"I've had pretty good success
against Stan Musial by throwing
him my best pitch ... and then
backing up third."*
— Carl Erskine

Free Baseball!

EXTRA INNINGS ARE always a bonus! This extra inning will give us the opportunity to dig even deeper into the Cardinals' rich history. Fasten your seat belt; this ride's not quite over. We've got another 20 miscellaneous questions to throw at you; all dealing with World Series engagements involving the Redbirds over the years. This should be informative and quite entertaining for diehard fans like you! Good luck!

TOP OF THE TENTH

QUESTION 181: Name the player who led the Cardinals with a .417 batting average in the 1926 World Series victory over the Yankees.
- a) Tommy Threvenow
- b) Les Bell
- c) Jim Bottomley
- d) Rogers Hornsby

QUESTION 182: Name the player who led the Cardinals with six runs scored in the '26 World Series.
- a) Jim Bottomley
- b) Billy Southworth
- c) Les Bell
- d) Taylor Douthit

QUESTION 183: The Cardinals were swept by the Yankees in four straight games in the 1928 World Series; what did the Redbirds hit as a team in that Fall Classic?
- a) .226
- b) .218
- c) .206
- d) .198

QUESTION 184: Who hit the only home run for the Cardinals in the '28 World Series?

a) Chick Hafey
b) Jim Bottomley
c) Frankie Frisch
d) Ernie Orsatti

QUESTION 185: Pepper Martin hit .500 for the Cardinals in the 1931 World Series victory over the Philadelphia Athletics; what was the next highest batting average on the team in that Series?
a) .273
b) .259
c) .286
d) .267

QUESTION 186: Name the player who led the Cardinals with six RBIs in the 1934 World Series victory over Detroit.
a) Jack Rothrock
b) Frankie Frisch
c) Joe Medwick
d) Ripper Collins

QUESTION 187: Name the pitcher who notched two wins in the 1942 World Series victory over the Yankees.
a) Max Lanier
b) Johnny Beazley
c) Mort Cooper
d) Ernie White

QUESTION 188: Name the player who led the Cardinals with three doubles in the 1944 World Series victory over the hometown rival Browns.
a) Marty Marion
b) Stan Musial
c) Whitey Kurowski
d) Walker Cooper

QUESTION 189: Name the player who hit the lone home run for the Cardinals in the seven-game World Series victory over the Red Sox in 1946.
- a) Stan Musial
- b) Terry Moore
- c) Enos Slaughter
- d) Whitey Kurowski

QUESTION 190: Name the pitcher who won three games in the 1946 World Series for the Cardinals.
- a) Harry Brecheen
- b) George Munger
- c) Al Brazle
- d) Murry Dickson

TOP OF THE TENTH ANSWER KEY

___ **QUESTION 181:** A
___ **QUESTION 182:** B
___ **QUESTION 183:** C
___ **QUESTION 184:** B
___ **QUESTION 185:** C
___ **QUESTION 186:** A
___ **QUESTION 187:** B
___ **QUESTION 188:** A
___ **QUESTION 189:** C
___ **QUESTION 190:** A

KEEP A RUNNING TALLY OF YOUR CORRECT ANSWERS!

Number correct: __ / 10

Overall correct: __ / 190

BOTTOM OF THE TENTH

QUESTION 191: Name the player who led the Cardinals with 11 hits in the 1964 World Series victory over the Yankees.
a) Ken Boyer
b) Mike Shannon
c) Curt Flood
d) Tim McCarver

QUESTION 192: Name the player who led the Cardinals with seven RBIs in the 1967 World Series victory over the Red Sox.
a) Lou Brock
b) Roger Maris
c) Julian Javier
d) Curt Flood

QUESTION 193: Name the player who led the Cardinals with six RBIs in the 1968 World Series defeat to the Tigers.
a) Lou Brock
b) Mike Shannon
c) Tim McCarver
d) Orlando Cepeda

QUESTION 194: How many combined bases did Lou Brock steal in the '67 and '68 World Series?
a) 10
b) 12
c) 14
d) 16

QUESTION 195: How many bases did Lou Brock steal in the 1964 World Series?
a) 2
b) 5
c) 0
d) 3

QUESTION 196: Name the player who had 9 hits in 17 at-bats for the Cardinals in the 1982 World Series victory over the Brewers.
   a) Darrell Porter
   b) Keith Hernandez
   c) George Hendrick
   d) Dan Iorg

QUESTION 197: Name the player who provided the only run of the game for the Cardinals with a ninth inning home run in Game 3 of the 2004 World Series loss to the Red Sox.
   a) Albert Pujols
   b) Larry Walker
   c) Jim Edmonds
   d) Edgar Renteria

QUESTION 198: Who made the last out of the 2004 World Series?
   a) Edgar Renteria
   b) Scott Rolen
   c) Tony Womack
   d) Reggie Sanders

QUESTION 199: Who was the winning pitcher for the Cardinals in Game 5 of the 2006 World Series over the Detroit Tigers?
   a) Jeff Weaver
   b) Adam Wainwright
   c) Chris Carpenter
   d) Anthony Reyes

QUESTION 200: Who pitched eight innings in Game 1 of the 2006 World Series, notching a win for the Cardinals over the Tigers, 7-2?
   a) Chris Carpenter
   b) Jeff Suppan
   c) Anthony Reyes
   d) Jason Marquis

Bottom of the Tenth Answer Key

___ **Question 191:** D
___ **Question 192:** B
___ **Question 193:** D
___ **Question 194:** C
___ **Question 195:** C
___ **Question 196:** D
___ **Question 197:** B
___ **Question 198:** A
___ **Question 199:** A
___ **Question 200:** C

Keep a running tally of your correct answers!

Number correct: ___ / 10

Overall correct: ___ / 200

"We thought we had good character, not just good talent. That means you can't quit and can't give up. We did get to the end, and a lot of it was our character. This one here has its own mark, because coming from that far back is historic."
— Tony La Russa, after the Cardinals won the 2011 Wild Card

2011 World Series Champions

THE CARDINALS TRAILED Milwaukee by ten games in the NL Central on August 25, 2011, and even more discouraging was the 10.5 game deficit to Atlanta that the Cardinals faced in the Wild Card chase. That frustration was completely erased on September 29, however, as the Cardinals completed one of the greatest comebacks in history to make the postseason. It took a lot of help from a Braves team that lost 20 of its final 31 games, but the Cardinals did their part, winning 23 of 32 to close out the regular season and claim the Wild Card berth on the season's final day.

But the fun was just starting for this club.

The Phillies and the Brewers were expected to meet in the NLCS, but the Cardinals spoiled their postseason plans as well, knocking off the Phillies first, and then taking care of the Brewers in the NLCS to claim the pennant and set up a showdown with the Texas Rangers in the 2011 World Series.

Enjoy these 30 bonus questions that celebrate the Cardinals success in 2011!

QUESTION 201: With one prolific week the first week of June, this slugger quieted early-season naysayers for good when he blasted five home runs, including four in three days. In seven games that week he was 12 for 27 at the plate, scored 11 runs, picked up ten RBIs, and totaled 29 bases ... and earned NL Player of the Week honors for his prodigious blasts. Pick the slugger who posted these gaudy numbers in June 2011—Lance Berkman or Albert Pujols?

QUESTION 202: This slugger batted 11 for 24 in six games during the third week of April 2011. He totaled 20 bases and posted a .833 slugging percentage with two homers, three doubles, and eight RBIs. And for his ridiculous assault on Astros pitching he was named the NL Player of the Week ... *for the second time in three weeks in the season's first month.* Pick the slugger who carried the Cardinals offense in the season's first month—Lance Berkman or Matt Holliday?

QUESTION 203: After going homerless with just one RBI in his first eight games in April 2011, this slugger got well at the expense of the Diamondbacks pitching staff and carried the Cardinals to a 5-2 record for the week. He led the majors with six home runs, 12 RBIs, and a 1.167 slugging percentage. He was 10 for 24 at the plate, hit his second career grand slam, and had a pair of multi-home run games in the week. Against the Dodgers he homered in consecutive at-bats, but adding to the offensive onslaught was Albert Pujols, who homered in consecutive at-bats in the same game ... it was the first time in franchise history that two players homered in consecutive at bats in the same game. And for the aforementioned slugger, it was the first of two Player of the Week honors earned in April 2011. So who was it—Lance Berkman or Matt Holiday?

QUESTION 204: The Cardinals sluggers weren't the only ones earning recognition for early season success. After losing consecutive games against the Padres to start the season, St. Louis turned to this starter on Sunday, April 3, to right the ship and get the season's first win. All he did was shutout the Padres while facing just four batters over the minimum, throwing 102 pitches, and striking out nine. He completed the four-hitter to seal a 2-0 win and for his strong performance was co-NL Player of the Week. The hurler was—Jaime Garcia or Chris Carpenter?

QUESTION 205: After winning the Wild Card by a single game on the season's final day, the aphorism "they all count" never felt more true ... but it was a 5-1 record and a season best .833 winning percentage against this team that made the Cardinals late-season heroics possible. With the exception of inter-league rival Baltimore (3-0, 1.000), against which team did the Cardinals post their best winning percentage during the 2011 regular season—San Diego Padres or Atlanta Braves?

QUESTION 206: Who was the Cardinals Opening Day Starter vs. the San Diego Padres on March 31, 2011? He made a quality start but the Cardinals fell to the Padres 5-3 in extra-innings. Six months and 161 games later, Tony La Russa had tweaked his rotation so this same pitcher would get the ball on the season's final day in case the Cardinals still had a shot at the Wild Card. The Cardinals did have a shot, and so the same guy who opened the season closed it out ... with a two-hit shutout vs. the Houston Astros. No doubt he was getting a W that day, he was dominant, and the Cardinals watched from the clubhouse 40 minutes later as the Braves fell in extra-innings to the Phillies, handing the Wild Card berth to St. Louis. Who started games 1 and 162 for the Cardinals—Chris Carpenter or Jaime Garcia?

QUESTION 207: As a team the Cardinals batted .273 in 2011, which ranked first out of 16 teams in the NL. Leading the way were guys like Albert Pujols (.299), Skip Schumaker (.283), David Freese (.297), and Lance Berkman (.301) ... but none of those guys were the team leader in average. So who did lead the Cardinals with a .305 batting average—Yadier Molina or Matt Holliday?

QUESTION 208: As a team the Cardinals also ranked first in runs, first in hits, third in doubles, and sixth in home runs among 16 NL teams. Two starting pitchers even got in the act, with Jaime Garcia and Jake Westbrook each going yard once— plus Chris Carpenter added three doubles. But among the guys who got paid to hit, who led the team in runs (105), hits (173), home runs (37), and RBIs (99)—Lance Berkman or Albert Pujols?

QUESTION 209: This Cardinals starter was at his best when the club needed him the most—facing deep deficits in the standings and needing a win every day to stay within striking distance of the Braves in the Wild Card chase, he posted a 5-1 record in August and September and the Cardinals were 8-2 in his final ten starts and he finished the season with a team high 14 wins. Who came up clutch for the Cardinals down the stretch—Kyle Lohse or Jaime Garcia?

QUESTION 210: Among the team's starting pitchers, only one posted an earned run average over 4.00 while two posted sub-3.50 earned run averages. Who led the club with a 3.39 earned run average—Chris Carpenter or Kyle Lohse?

> *"It was exciting, there's no doubt about it. The way these guys have played the past month and a half has been amazing, every single night grinding, playing their butts off, not giving up. We continued to give ourselves an opportunity and now we are here."*
> *— Chris Carpenter, after the Cardinals won the 2011 Wild Card*

QUESTION 211: Now for some postseason questions ... after dropping Game 1 of the NLDS 11-6 to the Phillies, the Cardinals fell into an early 4-0 hole with Cliff Lee on the mound in Game 2. The offense rallied, however, with three runs in the fourth, the tying run in the sixth, and after a leadoff triple by Allen Craig in the seventh, Albert Pujols singled in the winning run in the 5-4 final. It was the third time in his career that Pujols had a go-ahead RBI in the seventh inning or later of a Cardinals postseason game, setting a new franchise record that Pujols had previously shared with Brian Jordan and one other player. Who else in Cardinals history had two game-winning hits in the seventh inning or later of a postseason game—Willie McGee or Vince Coleman?

QUESTION 212: After earning a split in Philly, the Cardinals lost a tough Game 3 at home, 3-2. Facing elimination in a must-win Game 4, Tony La Russa gave the ball to Edwin Jackson. In his first career playoff start, he gave up two runs in his first five pitches—a double, a triple, and a single to the first three batters he faced. Jackson settled down, however, and when he left after six solid innings of work, the Cardinals held a 5-2 lead thanks to the bat of this teammate, who had a two-run double in the fourth and a two-run home run in the sixth. Who's big bat carried the day in Game 4—David Freese or Lance Berkman?

QUESTION 213: To advance to the NLCS the Cardinals had to beat Roy Halladay ... in Philly. The Cardinals scored the first, and as it turned out, only run of the game when this player battled through a ten-pitch at bat to deliver a run scoring double in the first inning. It was his longest at bat of the season and only the third time all year that any player had a plate appearance of at least ten pitches against Halladay. Who delivered the only run in the Cardinals 1-0 Game 5 victory— Matt Holliday or Skip Schumaker?

QUESTION 214: It's hard to believe one run stood up against the Phillies offense, but it did—thanks to this pitcher, who tossed a three-hit complete game shutout. He became just the sixth pitcher in three decades to toss a shutout in the deciding game of a postseason series, and the first to give up three hits or fewer since Sandy Koufax in the 1965 World Series. Who clinched the series for the Cardinals—Jaime Garcia or Chris Carpenter?

QUESTION 215: One of the five other pitchers to toss a shutout in the deciding game of a postseason series in the last three decades also pulled of this fantastic feat for the Cardinals. Who tossed a shutout vs. San Francisco in Game 7 of the 1987 NLCS—Danny Cox or John Tudor?

QUESTION 216: The final out of the 2011 NLDS vs. Philly was a grounder to second by this slugger ... who had also ended the Phillies 2010 NLDS vs. San Francisco when he struck out with the tying run on second base. Which big bat was the final out for the second consecutive season for the Phillies—Ryan Howard or Chase Utley?

"Actually, I don't know what to say."
– Phillies Manager Charlie Manuel, after losing to the Cardinals in the NLCS

QUESTION 217: The 2011 NLCS started much like the NLDS, with a 9-6 loss on the road in Milwaukee. And just like the NLDS, the Cardinals earned a split on the road with a Game 2 victory. This time it was the Albert Pujols show. Pujols was 4 for 5 with a home run, three doubles, and five RBIs as the Cardinals rolled to a 12-3 final. His four extra-base hits tied a postseason record for a single game, and it also was his second game of the 2011 postseason with at least three extra-base hits—which made him the first player in baseball history to have two such games in a single postseason. And finally ... his five RBIs gave him 42 career postseason RBIs, which broke the previous franchise record of 41 held by which player—Jim Edmonds or Scott Rolen?

QUESTION 218: Edwin Jackson started Game 2 and was staked to an early 5-0 lead by the Cardinals offense, but after giving up two runs in the fourth and then allowing two base runners in the fifth, Tony La Russa wasted no time going to the bullpen—which gave the 'W' to a reliever who faced just one batter, threw only one pitch, and induced an inning-ending double play to double his win total for the entire year ... that's right, the Game 2 winner had notched only one victory in relief during the regular season. Who is he—Lance Lynn or Trever Miller?

QUESTION 219: In Game 3 of the NLCS, Albert Pujols made history again when he became the fifth player to hit seven doubles in a single postseason. His RBI double in the first contributed to a four-run inning, and that's all the scoring the Cards would get or need, holding on for a 4-3 victory. It was also the fifth consecutive postseason game the Cardinals scored in the first inning, something no team had done since the 2004 Red Sox. It was a good night all-around for Cardinals fans, as Hall of Fame legends Stan Musial, Bob Gibson, Lou Brock, and Red Schoendienst were on hand for pregame ceremonies. And to conjure up some good karma for their home NLCS games, the Cardinals brought back this player to throw out the ceremonial first pitch ... he was the 2006 NLCS MVP for St. Louis. Who is he—Adam Wainwright or Jeff Suppan?

QUESTION 220: After splitting Games 4 and 5, the Cardinals headed back to Milwaukee needing just one win to clinch the pennant. In the regular season the Brewers led the league with 185 home runs and the Cardinals led the league with a .273 team batting average. It was the fifth time in history that the team with the league's most homers faced the team with the league's highest batting average in an LCS, but ... it was the first time the team with the highest average won, and in this case, the team with the highest average—the Cardinals—used their opponents calling card to win: the long ball. Three of them, in fact, en route to a 12-6 win—including a three-run shot in the first to get things going by this player, who won Series MVP honors. Who is he—David Freese or Albert Pujols?

> *"We believe. I think that's what you've got to do in this game. We got a group of guys with some talent, desire, and just a ton of heart."*
> *— David Freese, after beating the Brewers to win the NL Pennant*

QUESTION 221: Because the Cards were the NL Wild Card team, the Red Birds began the NLDS and the NLCS on the road—and were forced to overcome long odds to defeat the two powerhouses of the NL. But thanks to the NL victory in Phoenix during the 2011 All-Star Game, Game 1 of the World Series was in St. Louis. It was an exciting and victorious night for the Cards, as Chris Carpenter won his third consecutive start in the 2011 postseason, 3-2, but it was this player who came off the bench that delivered the biggest hit of the night ... his pinch-hit single in the sixth inning on a 1-2 pitch scored David Freese with the go-ahead run. It was the first time since 1995 that a pinch-hitter drove home the go-ahead run during Game 1 of the World Series. Who did this for the Cards—Nick Punto or Allen Craig?

QUESTION 222: In Game 2, the Rangers rallied for two ninth-inning runs to escape with a 2-1 victory and even the series a game apiece—but the Rangers had no chance to build on that momentum at home in Game 3 thanks to Albert Pujols, who paced the Cards offense in a 16-7 thrashing of the Rangers with five hits, three home runs, and six RBIs. He tied or set five single-game records that night—most home runs, hits, RBIs, total bases (14), and most consecutive innings with a hit (four). It was a much-less heralded player, however, who gave the Cards the first lead of the night for a record tenth consecutive game in a single postseason. Who hit a first inning home run to get the Cards offense on the board—Rafael Furcal or Allen Craig?

QUESTION 223: The offense disappeared for Games 4 and 5, as the Rangers won 4-0 and 4-2. The series shifted back to St. Louis for a must-win Game 6 ... and what a wild game it turned out to be. The Cards won 10-9 in 11 innings, after trailing by two runs in both the ninth and tenth innings, and being down to their final strike in both frames. However, this player saved the season when he hit a two-run, two-out triple to tie the game in the ninth, and a walk-off home run to win it in the 11th ... who is he—Lance Berkman or David Freese?

"If you watch the history of baseball, teams come back."
— Tony La Russa, after the Cardinals Game 6 rally

QUESTION 224: In Game 7, Josh Hamilton and Michael Young had first-inning RBI doubles to stake the Rangers to an early 2-0 lead. And like Game 6, that two-run deficit meant nothing to the Cardinals. Who scored the Cardinals first run of the game as the Red Birds came right back with two runs of their own in the home half of the first—Ryan Theriot or Albert Pujols?

QUESTION 225: Who hit a third-inning solo home run that proved to be the game-winner—Lance Berkman or Allen Craig?

QUESTION 226: For only the sixth time in baseball history, a pair of teammates both hit at least three home runs in the same World Series. Which pair did this for the 2011 Cardinals—Albert Pujols and David Freese or Albert Pujols and Allen Craig?

QUESTION 227: The Cards won 6-2 in Game 7, adding to the franchise's major league record for most Game 7 wins in World Series history. The Cardinals have lost Game 7 of the World Series three times ... but after beating the Rangers, how many times have the Cardinals won Game 7 of the World Series—six or eight?

> *"We tried to come back today, but the momentum just took them."*
> *– Rangers third baseman Adrian Beltre, on the Cardinals Game 7 victory*

QUESTION 228: When this player drew a bases loaded walk in the fifth inning, it gave the Cardinals a 4-2 lead and it made him just the third player in history to draw a pair of bases loaded walks in a single World Series. Who did this to earn a couple of easy RBIs vs. the Rangers—Yadier Molina or Lance Berkman?

QUESTION 229: Who set or tied three postseason records with 21 RBIs, 52 total bases, and 25 hits during the Cardinals remarkable run through October and for his exploits vs. the

Rangers also took home World Series MVP honors—David Freese or Albert Pujols?

QUESTION 230: It was fitting that this player took the mound to start and earned the win in Game 7. Who was it—Chris Carpenter or Jaime Garcia?

2011 WS Champions Answer Key

___ **Question 201:** Albert Pujols
___ **Question 202:** Lance Berkman
___ **Question 203:** Lance Berkman
___ **Question 204:** Jaime Garcia
___ **Question 205:** Atlanta Braves
___ **Question 206:** Chris Carpenter
___ **Question 207:** Yadier Molina
___ **Question 208:** Albert Pujols
___ **Question 209:** Kyle Lohse
___ **Question 210:** Kyle Lohse
___ **Question 211:** Vince Coleman
___ **Question 212:** David Freese
___ **Question 213:** Skip Schumaker
___ **Question 214:** Chris Carpenter
___ **Question 215:** Danny Cox
___ **Question 216:** Ryan Howard
___ **Question 217:** Jim Edmonds
___ **Question 218:** Lance Lynn
___ **Question 219:** Jeff Suppan
___ **Question 220:** David Freese
___ **Question 221:** Allen Craig
___ **Question 222:** Allen Craig
___ **Question 223:** David Freese
___ **Question 224:** Albert Pujols
___ **Question 225:** Allen Craig
___ **Question 226:** Albert Pujols and Allen Craig
___ **Question 227:** eight
___ **Question 228:** Yadier Molina
___ **Question 229:** David Freese
___ **Question 230:** Chris Carpenter

Keep a running tally of your correct answers!

Number correct: __ / 30

Overall correct: __ / 230

St. Louis Cardinals IQ

It's time to find out your Cardinals IQ. Add your total from all eleven chapters and see how you did! Here's how it breaks down:

GENIUS CARDINALS IQ EXCEEDS ALBERT PUJOLS	= 200-230
GENIUS CARDINALS IQ DESTINED TO BE A FIRST BALLOT HALL OF FAMER	= 180-199
GENIUS CARDINALS IQ IS WORTHY OF A WORLD CHAMPIONSHIP	= 170-179
SUPERIOR CARDINALS IQ IS WORTHY OF LEGENDARY STATUS	= 160-169
SUPERIOR CARDINALS IQ MAKES YOU ONE OF THE ALL-TIME GREATS	= 150-159
OUTSTANDING CARDINALS IQ THAT PLACES YOU AMONG THE TOP PLAYERS	= 140-149
ABOVE AVERAGE CARDINALS IQ THAT EARNS YOU A NICE PAYCHECK	= 130-139
SOLID CARDINALS IQ THAT LETS YOU PLAY BALL FOR A LIVING	= 120-129
AVERAGE CARDINALS IQ GOOD ENOUGH TO GET YOU TO THE SHOW	= 110-119
AVERAGE CARDINALS IQ GOT YOU A CUP OF COFFEE BUT THAT'S ALL	= 100-109

Thanks for taking the latest Ultimate Test of True Fandom! I hope you enjoyed taking this test as much as I enjoyed putting it together for Cards fans of all ages.

About the Author

LARRY UNDERWOOD grew up in St. Louis and has been following Cardinals baseball for over 50 years. After a 26-year career with Enterprise Rent-a-Car (1974-2000) as one of the Desert Southwest pioneers, Underwood retired, then several years later, wrote about his career experiences in the book, *Life Under the Corporate Microscope – A Maverick's Irreverent Perspective.* He has already published one other Cards trivia book: *St. Louis Cardinals IQ – The Ultimate Test of True Fandom – Volume I.* This is his third book, overall.

References

Nemec, David and Flatow, Scott, *Ultimate St. Louis Cardinals Baseball Challenge* (Lanham MD: Taylor Trade Publishing, 2008).

Snyder, John, *St. Louis Cardinals Journal* (Cincinnati OH: Clerisy Press, 2010).

Reichler, Joseph, *The Baseball Encyclopedia – The Complete and Official Record of Major League Baseball* (New York: MacMillan Publishing Co, Inc, 1979).

About Black Mesa

BLACK MESA IS a Florida-based publishing company that specializes in sports history and trivia books. Look for these popular titles in our trivia IQ series:

- *Mixed Martial Arts (Volumes I & II)*
- *Boston Red Sox (Volumes I & II)*
- *Tampa Bay Rays*
- *New York Yankees*
- *Atlanta Braves*
- *Milwaukee Brewers*
- *St.. Louis Cardinals Volume I (Larry Underwood)*
- *Major League Baseball*
- *Cincinnati Reds*
- *Texas Rangers*
- *Boston Celtics*
- *Florida Gators Football*
- *Georgia Bulldogs Football*
- *Texas Longhorns Football*
- *Oklahoma Sooners Football*
- *Texas A&M Aggies Football*
- *New England Patriots*
- *Buffalo Bills*

For information about special discounts for bulk purchases, please email:

black.mesa.publishing@gmail.com

www.blackmesabooks.com

Also in the Sports by the Numbers Series

- *Major League Baseball*
- *New York Yankees*
- *Boston Red Sox*
- *San Francisco Giants*
- *Texas Rangers*
- *University of Oklahoma Football*
- *University of Georgia Football*
- *Penn State University Football*
- *NASCAR*
- *Sacramento Kings*
- *Mixed Martial Arts*

The following is an excerpt from

St. Louis Cardinals IQ: The Ultimate Test of True Fandom

Larry Underwood

2010 Edition (Volume I)

Chapter One

SPRING TRAINING

THIS IS SPRING TRAINING MIND YOU. We're only stretching here. Just trying to get limber after a long winter of chips, couches, remote controls, beverages of choice, and the NFL ... I mean, there's no sense straining a groin or anything else right out of the box. So we'll just start with some basics – a few Cardinals legends and some numbers that go with them.

No point in sweating bullets over these questions. You don't know these, well, you don't know Jack (Buck?). Or Mike Shannon for that matter!

THE NUMBERS GAME

QUESTION 1: Stan Musial had 3,630 hits in his career. What was unusual about that total?
   a) He played the harmonica 3,630 times in the clubhouse after the games, as well
   b) He gave 3,630 post game interviews to Harry Caray
   c) Exactly half of his hits were at home, and half on the road
   d) He once used his harmonica to record one of his hits and the record went platinum.

QUESTION 2: How many home runs did Stan Musial hit during his career?
   a) 475
   b) 363
   c) 501
   d) 490

QUESTION 3: What number did Dizzy Dean wear while playing for the Cardinals?

a) 47
b) 37
c) 17
d) 27

QUESTION 4: In 1967, the Cardinals got off to a fast start, winning how many games in a row, before finally losing one?
a) 9
b) 6
c) 11
d) 8

QUESTION 5: In 1979, Keith Hernandez led the National League in batting and was named co-MVP. What was his batting average that season?
a) .341
b) .356
c) .323
d) .344

THE ROOKIES

QUESTION 6: Nicknamed "The Fulton Flash," he was once named the National League Rookie of the Year.
a) Ted Sizemore
b) Bill Virdon
c) Bake McBride
d) Wally Moon

QUESTION 7: This rookie pitcher won 16 games for the Cardinals in 1967.
a) Steve Carlton
b) Dick Hughes
c) Nelson Briles
d) Reggie Cleveland

QUESTION 8: This rookie first baseman was a disappointment for the Cardinals in 1970.
   a) Joe Hague
   b) Keith Hernandez
   c) Jose Cruz
   d) Reggie Smith

QUESTION 9: This slick fielding third baseman broke in with the Cardinals in 1972, hitting .359 in 21 games.
   a) Hector Cruz
   b) Ken Reitz
   c) Norman Mailer
   d) Gene Simmons

QUESTION 10: This rookie catcher once got four hits in a single World Series game.
   a) Branch Rickey
   b) Joe Garagiola
   c) Tom Nieto
   d) Jose Molina

THE VETERANS

QUESTION 11: This backup catcher helped the Cardinals win the World Series in 1982.
   a) Steve Lake
   b) Gene Tenace
   c) Tom Nieto
   d) Dave Ricketts

QUESTION 12: In the final inning of the 1985 NLCS, Dodger manager Tom Lasorda elected to pitch to this Cardinals slugger, with first base open and Andy Van Slyke on deck.
   a) David Green
   b) Bob Horner
   c) Jack Clark
   d) Pedro Guerrero

QUESTION 13: This Whitey Herzog early free agent acquisition was a bust during the regular season, but a two-time MVP in the postseason.
a) George Hendrick
b) Tom Lawless
c) Darryl Porter
d) Tom Pagnozzi

QUESTION 14: This consistent third baseman once hit exactly 24 home runs per season for four consecutive seasons.
a) Ken Reitz
b) Joe Torre
c) Ken Boyer
d) Mike Shannon

QUESTION 15: This slugger was traded to the Dodgers for Ted Sizemore.
a) Reggie Smith
b) Dick Allen
c) Art Shamsky
d) Pedro Guerrero

Note: Spring Training is gearing up for the regular season. No more, easy "multiple choice" questions!

THE LEGENDS

QUESTION 16: Who was the last National League player to win the Triple Crown?

QUESTION 17: Who did Nelson Briles replace in the starting rotation after a broken leg suffered on July 15, 1967 put him on the disabled list for eight weeks?

QUESTION 18: What player was nearly traded to the Philadelphia Phillies for pitcher Robin Roberts in 1958?

QUESTION 19: Whose home run in the bottom of the 12th gave the National League a 6-5 victory over the American League in the 1955 All-Star Game at Milwaukee's County Stadium?

QUESTION 20: With the Cardinals trailing the Yankees in the World Series 2 games to 1, and down 3-0 in the game, his grand slam home run turned the tide for the Cardinals in the 1964 World Series. Who hit this clutch home run?

THE HITTERS

QUESTION 21: What player's .358 lifetime batting average is second only to Ty Cobb's .367?

QUESTION 22: This power hitting first baseman's nickname was "The Big Cat." Name him.

QUESTION 23: Who's the only player in Major League history to have two grand slam home runs in the same inning, off the same pitcher, no less?

QUESTION 24: Despite hitting fewer than ten home runs in 1985, this clutch hitter drove in 110 runs for the pennant-winning Cardinals in 1985.

QUESTION 25: This legendary game-winning grand slam gave the Cardinals an extra-inning 7-6 victory over Houston, on May 1, 1979. Who hit it?

Chapter One Answer Key

Time to find out how you did – put a check mark next to the questions you answered correctly, and when you are done be sure to add up you score to find out your IQ, and to find out if you made the Opening Day roster!

THE NUMBERS GAME

___QUESTION 1: C – Musial was the model of consistency during his career, spreading his hits evenly between home and away games – 1,815 apiece.

___QUESTION 2: A – Musial had 475 career home runs.

___QUESTION 3: C – Dizzy Dean wore number 17.

___QUESTION 4: B – The Cards won their first six games in 1967.

___QUESTION 5: D – Hernandez hit .344 in 1979.

THE ROOKIES

___QUESTION 6: C – Bake McBride was nicknamed "The Fulton Flash" by broadcaster Mike Shannon, en route to winning the 1974 NL Rookie of the Year award.

___QUESTION 7: B – Dick Hughes won 16 games for the Cardinals as a 29-year-old rookie in 1967. The following season, an arm injury ended his brief career.

___QUESTION 8: A – The Cardinals were expecting big things from their rookie first baseman in 1970, but Joe Hague was a disappointment, with only 14 home runs.

___**QUESTION 9:** B – Ken Reitz hit an impressive .359 in limited play in 1972. That was a fluke for one of the slowest players in the history of the game.

___**QUESTION 10:** B – Rookie catcher Joe Garagiola banged out four hits in Game 3 of the 1946 World Series. Meanwhile, Joe's neighborhood pal Yogi Berra was embarking on a Hall of Fame career with the New York Yankees. They just had to sign Garagiola?

THE VETERANS

___**QUESTION 11:** B – Ten years after starring in the '72 World Series for Oakland, Gene Tenace provided much needed bench support in helping the Cards reach the Promised Land in '82.

___**QUESTION 12:** C – Jack Clark wasn't called "Jack the Ripper" for nothing, as he ripped a first pitch fastball over the left field fence for a pennant-clinching home run in '85, against a poorly managed Dodger team.

___**QUESTION 13:** C – Darryl Porter didn't have much to write home about during the regular season, but his bat came alive in the postseason to help the Cards win the '82 World Series over the Milwaukee Brewers.

___**QUESTION 14:** C – Ken Boyer had pretty good power and won a NL MVP award in '64, helping the Cards win the World Series, but his consistency was remarkable; 24 home runs for four consecutive years in the '60s!

___**QUESTION 15:** B – After the '69 season, the Cards figured they needed some power, so they acquired Dick Allen from the Phillies; he responded with 34 home runs and 101 runs batted in. Naturally, the front office then decided they didn't need all that power after all, and traded him for a singles hitter – Ted Sizemore, after the season ended.

THE LEGENDS

___QUESTION 16: Albert Pujols hasn't quite done it yet; but he probably will win the Triple Crown before his career is over. As it stands right now, the last NL player to accomplish that feat is none other than Joe "Ducky" Medwick, way back in 1937.

___QUESTION 17: In July of '67, Roberto Clemente hit a vicious line drive off Bob Gibson's right leg, causing a slight fracture just below the knee cap. Gibson would be shelved for a couple of months, but came back stronger than ever to power the Cardinals past the Red Sox in the World Series. In the meantime, Nelson Briles stepped into the starting rotation after Gibby went down, and pitched brilliantly, proving to be a rising star.

___QUESTION 18: While Frank Lane was the Cardinals' General Manager back in the late '50s, he tried to swing a deal which would send Stan Musial to Philadelphia, in exchange for pitcher Robin Roberts. Ownership vetoed the deal, and "Trader Lane" was sent packing, shortly thereafter.

___QUESTION 19: Speak of the Devil! It was none other than Stan Musial who hit the dramatic, game-winning home run in the '55 All-Star Game in Milwaukee.

___QUESTION 20: Ken Boyer was the hero in Game 4 of the '64 World Series. Boyer's blast, a dramatic grand slam home run off Yankees pitcher Al Downing, turned a 3-0 deficit into a 4-3 victory.

THE HITTERS

___QUESTION 21: Rogers Hornsby, who played for the Cardinals from 1915 to 1926, and then again briefly in 1933, recorded the second highest lifetime batting average of all-time. With his .358 mark, only Cobb was better.

___QUESTION 22: This is a tricky one. Andres Gallaraga spent one injury plagued season with the Cardinals (1992) before heading to the hitter friendly confines of Coors Field; but his nickname was "The Cat"; not "The Big Cat"; that nickname belonged to Hall of Fame slugger Johnny Mize, who played for the Cardinals from 1936 to 1941. If you got that one correct, you're probably going to go far in this league!

___QUESTION 23: Free-swinging third baseman Fernando Tatis is the only player in MLB history to hit two grand slam home runs in the same inning; and he'll probably be the only one to do it for the next 1,000 years or so. As a footnote to this amazing feat, Tatis connected off the same pitcher for both big blows – Chan Ho Park – who probably wishes he would've been pulled after the first third-inning dinger! The date of this historic performance: April 23, 1999. The location: Dodger Stadium.

___QUESTION 24: In 1985, second baseman Tom Herr accomplished the rare feat of driving in over 100 runs in a season (110), without making it to double digits in home runs (8). With guys like Vince Coleman and Willie McGee always on base, and frequently in scoring position, all Tommy had to do was hit a line drive somewhere; he did, with great proficiency!

___QUESTION 25: Pinch-hitter Roger Freed connected on a 3-2 fastball thrown by Houston reliever Joe Sambito with two outs and the bases loaded in the bottom of the 11th inning; turning a 6-3 deficit into a stunning 7-6 Cardinals win.

Want to read more?

St. Louis Cardinals IQ:
The Ultimate Test of True Fandom
(Volume I)

Available at your favorite online retailer
and from the publisher at:

www.blackmesabooks.com

Made in the USA
Lexington, KY
24 May 2012